Journal With Grace

SARAH M. GRACE

Copyright © 2020 Sarah Grace

First published 2020 by Sarah Grace Publishing
an imprint of Malcolm Down Publishing Ltd
www.malcolmdown.co.uk

24 23 22 21 20   7 6 5 4 3 2 1

The right of Sarah Grace to be identified as the author of this work has
been asserted by her in accordance with the Copyright, Designs and
Patents Act 1988.

British Library Cataloguing in Publication Data

A catalogue record for this book is available from the British Library.

ISBN 978-1-912863-30-3

Cover design by Emily Markwick
Art direction by Sarah Grace

Interior design and typesetting by 2K/DENMARK
Set at 11 and 28 pts. in Grace Dyslexic designed by 2K/DENMARK

Printed in the UK

Introduction to Gracelets

Hopefully you have bought this journal with the accompanying book 'Journey with Grace' by Sarah Grace.

Gracelets within this book are taken from the end of each chapter of 'Journey with Grace' and will travel through this journal, like little gems, gifts that we can keep hold of.

Sarah Grace is a psychotherapist and counsellor who encourages and enjoys journalling.

A note from the author:

There is something very powerful about seeing our thoughts on paper. It can help to make more sense of things. It is also good to hear ourselves say things out loud.

During counselling sessions, I often hear both children and adults say things that seem to surprise them. This is a moment of recognising what is going on subconsciously. Journalling is a wonderfully private moment in which we can make further connections.

I became fascinated with the idea of the journal as I saw how it linked with journey. Journey means 'to travel on a defined route', 'one's path in life'. It comes from the old French JOURNÉE, meaning 'a day's length'. The Vulgar Latin DIUNUM, 'day', is a noun use of the neuter of Latin DIUNUM, meaning 'of one day', which in turn comes from the PIE (Proto-Indo- European) root dyeu meaning 'to shine'.

I played with this in my mind for a while and realised that really we only have the day in which to shine, and then it dies. We do not get that chance again, but if we are fortunate enough to have another, and another, we can continue to shine each day.

As we learn to live in the moment, feeling fully alive, we can learn from the day as it ends. As it dies, we can reflect on it, try to process it and learn from it. Another day comes . . . for some, although for some it ends, and there is no guarantee how many days we will get.

This has become a reality for many as we faced the coronavirus, and we have all recognised the stark truth of how vulnerable we are. No amount of money or status in society can keep us protected; we only have the day in which we live to be thankful for all we have.

It is hard to live as though we will not be alive tomorrow, as we live in a world of planning ahead. Yet there is tremendous value in being aware of and holding a moment in time that we can enjoy and treasure, even if it is not a huge moment. Seeing a feather float by or spotting a child playing in the leaves is a moment to hold on to.

Journalling is really helpful, even if it is sporadic; it can help us see things for what they are. As we journey on, it shows us how far we have come. In the difficult days it is easy to forget the good, and we often don't remember the wonderful things others say about us.

It is hard to get started sometimes, as it can feel like a chore, but even just writing some notes here and there will help to make sense of your thoughts along the way. Later, it becomes a wonderful gift to look back and see the journey you have travelled.

Enjoy your journalling journey!

Additional Services from Sarah Grace

For further help please email me on sarah@sarahmgrace.co.uk and title your emails specifically:

Creative Therapy | Play Therapy
Dyslexic Business Advice | Dyslexic Personal Support

Journalling
allows us to see
the journey so far,
enabling us to see
more clearly
where to go
from here.

Being curious
about ourselves
and others
opens up our minds,
allowing others
to do the same.

Through
tough times,
keep calm
and keep on
journalling!

The fear
of what we may find
is far more powerful
than its reality.
You are uniquely
and wonderfully made
so you may be nicely
surprised.

Remaining
with the pain
of the past,
because it is known,
can become safe.
Finding the strength
and true grit to move
from this place
means you will not
need to look back
any more.

There is
much more beyond
the now.

Life is a risk
– we have to
allow ourselves
to be vulnerable
to grow
in intimacy.

To allow you in –
I need to allow you
to see me
– intimacy –
'in to me you see'.

We only have
this day in which
to shine.

We can change
the narrative
by listening to
the thoughts we have;
being aware of them
and as we
understand them,
we have power
over them.

Push your desires
into the screen
of your heart,
that is where things
come into being.
Speaking them out
is where we can start
to live it out.

Why settle for
less than the best?
Instead allow yourself
to conceive, perceive
and believe
for more.

Bless yourself
and others
with the gift
of being
in the moment.

Being
in the moment and
allowing the feelings
to come through
creates space
for new dreams
and desires
that have been buried
or not yet born.

The ripple effect out
from being
in the moment
allows others
to be there with you.

Carve out time alone
and allow space
for reflection.

Making space
can lead us back
to ourselves
and others.

What better gift
is there
than really feeling alive
and being able to
encourage someone else
to feel the same!

Does what
you are doing
make sense,
bring meaning
and bring gratitude
to you or others?

What does the background noise sound like for you?

Does comparison
hold you back
or draw you away
from what you are
created to do?

We are designed
to fully live,
to live in full colour,
are your true colours
shining through?

We are quite often more fearful of what we are capable of than what we are not capable of.

Become
better acquainted
with ourselves
so when something new
comes along
we can face it,
capture it and make
peace with it.

Hope deferred
sickens the heart.
Let's allow hope
to shine through,
and the brokenness
become our way
to restore and
strengthen.

Find the thing that helps you just 'be'.

You can be successful
– it's only you
who is in the way
from seeing it.

Turn your weaknesses
into strengths,
use your secret weapon
and go for it!

God has made you
'uniquely you',
he knows the plans
he has for you.
So why not ask him?

Being real
and cultivating
an environment
you can flourish in
creates a better you
that ripples out better
for others.

Seeing
each other's strengths
and building
each other up
we could see
a better world
around us.

Celebrating
can be done daily;
appreciating each other
and small things.
These are easy to do
and yet easily missed.

We are
more than gold –
we are worth
so very much more
than we realise.

Living fully free
on the inside
can lead to the
empowerment of others
doing the same.

Allow yourself
the privilege of
fully living...

Further Help

Counselling

If you feel there are areas of your life that you would benefit from exploring in a deeper way, I would recommend talking to a counsellor.
Association of Christian Counsellors (ACC) www.acc-uk.org
British Association of Counsellors and Practitioners (BACP) www.bacp.co.uk

Counselling Directory

Making Contact

If you would like to contact me with regards to exploring the possibility of counselling, please contact me adding Counselling to the subject line:
grace4counselling@gmail.com | www.sarahmgrace.co.uk

Sarah Grace
Psychotherapist/Counsellor
Post Graduate Diploma in Contemporary Therapeutic Counselling
Professional registered member of the British Association of Counsellors and Psychotherapists. (Reg. M.B.A.C.P)

Retreats

Please email me on sarah@sarahmgrace.co.uk and title your email 'Retreat'.
Please email to ask for specific requirements as these can be discussed and tailored to your requirements.